SO-BRW-263
40

One times table

Here comes the one times table, it's lots of fun! Let's sing along, one by one.

$$0 \times 1 = 0$$
$$1 \times 1 = 1$$
$$2 \times 1 = 2$$
$$3 \times 1 = 3$$
$$4 \times 1 = 4$$
$$5 \times 1 = 5$$
$$6 \times 1 = 6$$
$$7 \times 1 = 7$$
$$8 \times 1 = 8$$
$$9 \times 1 = 9$$
$$10 \times 1 = 10$$
$$11 \times 1 = 11$$
$$12 \times 1 = 12$$

Two times table

Now you've reached times table number two! Wiggle and giggle, it's fun to do.

0 × 2 = 0
1 × 2 = 2
2 × 2 = 4
3 × 2 = 6
4 × 2 = 8
5 × 2 = 10
6 × 2 = 12
7 × 2 = 14
8 × 2 = 16
9 × 2 = 18
10 × 2 = 20
11 × 2 = 22
12 × 2 = 24

Three times table

Whoah, watch out for times table number three. Shimmy and shake – let's get funky!

$$0 \times 3 = 0$$
$$1 \times 3 = 3$$
$$2 \times 3 = 6$$
$$3 \times 3 = 9$$
$$4 \times 3 = 12$$
$$5 \times 3 = 15$$
$$6 \times 3 = 18$$
$$7 \times 3 = 21$$
$$8 \times 3 = 24$$
$$9 \times 3 = 27$$
$$10 \times 3 = 30$$
$$11 \times 3 = 33$$
$$12 \times 3 = 36$$

Four times table

Now you're at times table number four. Boogie and woogie – let's hit the dance floor!

$0 \times 4 = 0$

$1 \times 4 = 4$

$2 \times 4 = 8$

$3 \times 4 = 12$

$4 \times 4 = 16$

$5 \times 4 = 20$

$6 \times 4 = 24$

$7 \times 4 = 28$

$8 \times 4 = 32$

$9 \times 4 = 36$

$10 \times 4 = 40$

$11 \times 4 = 44$

$12 \times 4 = 48$

Five times table

Now you're at times table number five. Time to jump, jiggle and jive!

$$0 \times 5 = 0$$
$$1 \times 5 = 5$$
$$2 \times 5 = 10$$
$$3 \times 5 = 15$$
$$4 \times 5 = 20$$
$$5 \times 5 = 25$$
$$6 \times 5 = 30$$
$$7 \times 5 = 35$$
$$8 \times 5 = 40$$
$$9 \times 5 = 45$$
$$10 \times 5 = 50$$
$$11 \times 5 = 55$$
$$12 \times 5 = 60$$

Six times table

At the six times table, you're halfway there! Sing and dance – let down your hair!

$$0 \times 6 = 0$$
$$1 \times 6 = 6$$
$$2 \times 6 = 12$$
$$3 \times 6 = 18$$
$$4 \times 6 = 24$$
$$5 \times 6 = 30$$
$$6 \times 6 = 36$$
$$7 \times 6 = 42$$
$$8 \times 6 = 48$$
$$9 \times 6 = 54$$
$$10 \times 6 = 60$$
$$11 \times 6 = 66$$
$$12 \times 6 = 72$$

Seven times table

Here it comes, the seven times table. Stomp and stamp as loud as you're able!

$$0 \times 7 = 0$$
$$1 \times 7 = 7$$
$$2 \times 7 = 14$$
$$3 \times 7 = 21$$
$$4 \times 7 = 28$$
$$5 \times 7 = 35$$
$$6 \times 7 = 42$$
$$7 \times 7 = 49$$
$$8 \times 7 = 56$$
$$9 \times 7 = 63$$
$$10 \times 7 = 70$$
$$11 \times 7 = 77$$
$$12 \times 7 = 84$$

Eight times table

Wow, you're already at times table number eight! To get this far, you're doing just great!

$$0 \times 8 = 0$$
$$1 \times 8 = 8$$
$$2 \times 8 = 16$$
$$3 \times 8 = 24$$
$$4 \times 8 = 32$$
$$5 \times 8 = 40$$
$$6 \times 8 = 48$$
$$7 \times 8 = 56$$
$$8 \times 8 = 64$$
$$9 \times 8 = 72$$
$$10 \times 8 = 80$$
$$11 \times 8 = 88$$
$$12 \times 8 = 96$$

Nine times table

Now you've reached times table number nine. Sway and swing, and step in time!

$0 \times 9 = 0$

$1 \times 9 = 9$

$2 \times 9 = 18$

$3 \times 9 = 27$

$4 \times 9 = 36$

$5 \times 9 = 45$

$6 \times 9 = 54$

$7 \times 9 = 63$

$8 \times 9 = 72$

$9 \times 9 = 81$

$10 \times 9 = 90$

$11 \times 9 = 99$

$12 \times 9 = 108$

Ten times table

Whoah, watch out, it's times table number ten. Bop up and down – let's do it again!

0 × 10 = 0

1 × 10 = 10

2 × 10 = 20

3 × 10 = 30

4 × 10 = 40

5 × 10 = 50

6 × 10 = 60

7 × 10 = 70

8 × 10 = 80

9 × 10 = 90

10 × 10 = 100

11 × 10 = 110

12 × 10 = 120

Eleven times table

At the eleven times table, you're almost done. Just look at how far you've come!

$0 \times 11 = 0$

$1 \times 11 = 11$

$2 \times 11 = 22$

$3 \times 11 = 33$

$4 \times 11 = 44$

$5 \times 11 = 55$

$6 \times 11 = 66$

$7 \times 11 = 77$

$8 \times 11 = 88$

$9 \times 11 = 99$

$10 \times 11 = 110$

$11 \times 11 = 121$

$12 \times 11 = 132$

Twelve times table

Twirl and whirl, and leap and bend. At the twelve times table, you've sung along to the very end!

$$0 \times 12 = 0$$
$$1 \times 12 = 12$$
$$2 \times 12 = 24$$
$$3 \times 12 = 36$$
$$4 \times 12 = 48$$
$$5 \times 12 = 60$$
$$6 \times 12 = 72$$
$$7 \times 12 = 84$$
$$8 \times 12 = 96$$
$$9 \times 12 = 108$$
$$10 \times 12 = 120$$
$$11 \times 12 = 132$$
$$12 \times 12 = 144$$

Take a pencil and fill in the answers to each question in the following quizzes. Ask a grown-up to tick all the right answers (or check against the tables earlier in the book yourself!).
If you don't get your answers right the first time, don't worry. Just keep practising your tables and try again later.

Two times table quiz

2 x 2 = ____	7 x 2 = ____	12 x 2 = ____
10 x 2 = ____	3 x 2 = ____	0 x 2 = ____
1 x 2 = ____	11 x 2 = ____	4 x 2 = ____
6 x 2 = ____	2 x 2 = ____	8 x 2 = ____
0 x 2 = ____	10 x 2 = ____	3 x 2 = ____
4 x 2 = ____	0 x 2 = ____	9 x 2 = ____
3 x 2 = ____	5 x 2 = ____	5 x 2 = ____
7 x 2 = ____	1 x 2 = ____	2 x 2 = ____
12 x 2 = ____	4 x 2 = ____	6 x 2 = ____
9 x 2 = ____	8 x 2 = ____	10 x 2 = ____
5 x 2 = ____	6 x 2 = ____	1 x 2 = ____
11 x 2 = ____	9 x 2 = ____	7 x 2 = ____
8 x 2 = ____	12 x 2 = ____	11 x 2 = ____

Total ticks

Quiz comments

39 ticks:	congratulations! You're a whiz at this quiz!
34-38 ticks:	excellent
29-33 ticks:	great
24-28 ticks:	good
less than 24 ticks:	keep practising. You'll get there!

Three times table quiz

3 x 3 = ____	9 x 3 = ____	10 x 3 = ____
11 x 3 = ____	5 x 3 = ____	1 x 3 = ____
2 x 3 = ____	0 x 3 = ____	7 x 3 = ____
7 x 3 = ____	4 x 3 = ____	9 x 3 = ____
1 x 3 = ____	12 x 3 = ____	5 x 3 = ____
5 x 3 = ____	2 x 3 = ____	8 x 3 = ____
4 x 3 = ____	7 x 3 = ____	6 x 3 = ____
8 x 3 = ____	3 x 3 = ____	3 x 3 = ____
0 x 3 = ____	6 x 3 = ____	4 x 3 = ____
10 x 3 = ____	10 x 3 = ____	12 x 3 = ____
6 x 3 = ____	8 x 3 = ____	0 x 3 = ____
12 x 3 = ____	11 x 3 = ____	2 x 3 = ____
9 x 3 = ____	1 x 3 = ____	11 x 3 = ____

Total ticks

Quiz comments

39 ticks:	congratulations! You're a whiz at this quiz!
34-38 ticks:	excellent
29-33 ticks:	great
24-28 ticks:	good
less than 24 ticks:	keep practising. You'll get there!

Four times table quiz

5 x 4 = ___ ☆	6 x 4 = ___ ☆	11 x 4 = ___ ☆
10 x 4 = ___ ☆	1 x 4 = ___ ☆	2 x 4 = ___ ☆
0 x 4 = ___ ☆	11 x 4 = ___ ☆	8 x 4 = ___ ☆
4 x 4 = ___ ☆	5 x 4 = ___ ☆	7 x 4 = ___ ☆
9 x 4 = ___ ☆	10 x 4 = ___ ☆	9 x 4 = ___ ☆
3 x 4 = ___ ☆	0 x 4 = ___ ☆	6 x 4 = ___ ☆
7 x 4 = ___ ☆	3 x 4 = ___ ☆	4 x 4 = ___ ☆
6 x 4 = ___ ☆	8 x 4 = ___ ☆	0 x 4 = ___ ☆
12 x 4 = ___ ☆	4 x 4 = ___ ☆	5 x 4 = ___ ☆
2 x 4 = ___ ☆	7 x 4 = ___ ☆	10 x 4 = ___ ☆
8 x 4 = ___ ☆	9 x 4 = ___ ☆	1 x 4 = ___ ☆
11 x 4 = ___ ☆	2 x 4 = ___ ☆	3 x 4 = ___ ☆
1 x 4 = ___ ☆	12 x 4 = ___ ☆	12 x 4 = ___ ☆

Total ticks ☆

Quiz comments

39 ticks:	congratulations! You're a whiz at this quiz!
34-38 ticks:	excellent
29-33 ticks:	great
24-28 ticks:	good
less than 24 ticks:	keep practising. You'll get there!

Five times table quiz

6 x 5 = ____	8 x 5 = ____	10 x 5 = ____
10 x 5 = ____	3 x 5 = ____	0 x 5 = ____
1 x 5 = ____	7 x 5 = ____	9 x 5 = ____
5 x 5 = ____	2 x 5 = ____	6 x 5 = ____
4 x 5 = ____	12 x 5 = ____	8 x 5 = ____
8 x 5 = ____	5 x 5 = ____	5 x 5 = ____
7 x 5 = ____	6 x 5 = ____	7 x 5 = ____
3 x 5 = ____	9 x 5 = ____	4 x 5 = ____
0 x 5 = ____	0 x 5 = ____	2 x 5 = ____
11 x 5 = ____	11 x 5 = ____	11 x 5 = ____
9 x 5 = ____	1 x 5 = ____	3 x 5 = ____
12 x 5 = ____	10 x 5 = ____	1 x 5 = ____
2 x 5 = ____	4 x 5 = ____	12 x 5 = ____

Total ticks

Quiz comments

39 ticks:	congratulations! You're a whiz at this quiz!
34-38 ticks:	excellent
29-33 ticks:	great
24-28 ticks:	good
less than 24 ticks:	keep practising. You'll get there!

Six times table quiz

5 x 6 = _____ ☆	6 x 6 = _____ ☆	11 x 6 = _____ ☆
11 x 6 = _____ ☆	1 x 6 = _____ ☆	2 x 6 = _____ ☆
4 x 6 = _____ ☆	11 x 6 = _____ ☆	8 x 6 = _____ ☆
9 x 6 = _____ ☆	5 x 6 = _____ ☆	7 x 6 = _____ ☆
3 x 6 = _____ ☆	10 x 6 = _____ ☆	9 x 6 = _____ ☆
7 x 6 = _____ ☆	0 x 6 = _____ ☆	6 x 6 = _____ ☆
6 x 6 = _____ ☆	3 x 6 = _____ ☆	4 x 6 = _____ ☆
2 x 6 = _____ ☆	8 x 6 = _____ ☆	0 x 6 = _____ ☆
12 x 6 = _____ ☆	4 x 6 = _____ ☆	5 x 6 = _____ ☆
8 x 6 = _____ ☆	7 x 6 = _____ ☆	10 x 6 = _____ ☆
1 x 6 = _____ ☆	9 x 6 = _____ ☆	1 x 6 = _____ ☆
10 x 6 = _____ ☆	2 x 6 = _____ ☆	3 x 6 = _____ ☆
0 x 6 = _____ ☆	12 x 6 = _____ ☆	12 x 6 = _____ ☆

Total ticks ☆

Quiz comments

39 ticks:	congratulations! You're a whiz at this quiz!
34-38 ticks:	excellent
29-33 ticks:	great
24-28 ticks:	good
less than 24 ticks:	keep practising. You'll get there!

Seven times table quiz

1 x 7 = ____ ☆	3 x 7 = ____ ☆	10 x 7 = ____ ☆
10 x 7 = ____ ☆	2 x 7 = ____ ☆	9 x 7 = ____ ☆
7 x 7 = ____ ☆	7 x 7 = ____ ☆	5 x 7 = ____ ☆
9 x 7 = ____ ☆	1 x 7 = ____ ☆	0 x 7 = ____ ☆
5 x 7 = ____ ☆	12 x 7 = ____ ☆	4 x 7 = ____ ☆
8 x 7 = ____ ☆	5 x 7 = ____ ☆	2 x 7 = ____ ☆
6 x 7 = ____ ☆	4 x 7 = ____ ☆	7 x 7 = ____ ☆
3 x 7 = ____ ☆	8 x 7 = ____ ☆	3 x 7 = ____ ☆
4 x 7 = ____ ☆	0 x 7 = ____ ☆	6 x 7 = ____ ☆
11 x 7 = ____ ☆	11 x 7 = ____ ☆	11 x 7 = ____ ☆
0 x 7 = ____ ☆	6 x 7 = ____ ☆	8 x 7 = ____ ☆
12 x 7 = ____ ☆	10 x 7 = ____ ☆	1 x 7 = ____ ☆
2 x 7 = ____ ☆	9 x 7 = ____ ☆	12 x 7 = ____ ☆

Total ticks ☆

Quiz comments

39 ticks:	congratulations! You're a whiz at this quiz!
34-38 ticks:	excellent
29-33 ticks:	great
24-28 ticks:	good
less than 24 ticks:	keep practising. You'll get there!

Eight times table quiz

6 x 8 = ____ ☆	5 x 8 = ____ ☆	11 x 8 = ____ ☆
12 x 8 = ____ ☆	0 x 8 = ____ ☆	2 x 8 = ____ ☆
1 x 8 = ____ ☆	11 x 8 = ____ ☆	8 x 8 = ____ ☆
5 x 8 = ____ ☆	4 x 8 = ____ ☆	7 x 8 = ____ ☆
0 x 8 = ____ ☆	10 x 8 = ____ ☆	9 x 8 = ____ ☆
3 x 8 = ____ ☆	9 x 8 = ____ ☆	6 x 8 = ____ ☆
8 x 8 = ____ ☆	3 x 8 = ____ ☆	4 x 8 = ____ ☆
4 x 8 = ____ ☆	7 x 8 = ____ ☆	0 x 8 = ____ ☆
11 x 8 = ____ ☆	6 x 8 = ____ ☆	5 x 8 = ____ ☆
9 x 8 = ____ ☆	2 x 8 = ____ ☆	10 x 8 = ____ ☆
2 x 8 = ____ ☆	8 x 8 = ____ ☆	1 x 8 = ____ ☆
10 x 8 = ____ ☆	1 x 8 = ____ ☆	3 x 8 = ____ ☆
7 x 8 = ____ ☆	12 x 8 = ____ ☆	12 x 8 = ____ ☆

Total ticks ☆

Quiz comments

39 ticks:	congratulations! You're a whiz at this quiz!
34-38 ticks:	excellent
29-33 ticks:	great
24-28 ticks:	good
less than 24 ticks:	keep practising. You'll get there!

Nine times table quiz

0 x 9 = ____ ☆	6 x 9 = ____ ☆	10 x 9 = ____ ☆
10 x 9 = ____ ☆	1 x 9 = ____ ☆	8 x 9 = ____ ☆
6 x 9 = ____ ☆	5 x 9 = ____ ☆	3 x 9 = ____ ☆
8 x 9 = ____ ☆	4 x 9 = ____ ☆	7 x 9 = ____ ☆
5 x 9 = ____ ☆	12 x 9 = ____ ☆	2 x 9 = ____ ☆
7 x 9 = ____ ☆	8 x 9 = ____ ☆	5 x 9 = ____ ☆
4 x 9 = ____ ☆	7 x 9 = ____ ☆	6 x 9 = ____ ☆
2 x 9 = ____ ☆	3 x 9 = ____ ☆	9 x 9 = ____ ☆
3 x 9 = ____ ☆	0 x 9 = ____ ☆	0 x 9 = ____ ☆
11 x 9 = ____ ☆	11 x 9 = ____ ☆	11 x 9 = ____ ☆
9 x 9 = ____ ☆	9 x 9 = ____ ☆	4 x 9 = ____ ☆
12 x 9 = ____ ☆	10 x 9 = ____ ☆	1 x 9 = ____ ☆
1 x 9 = ____ ☆	2 x 9 = ____ ☆	12 x 9 = ____ ☆

Total ticks ☆

Quiz comments

39 ticks:	congratulations! You're a whiz at this quiz!
34-38 ticks:	excellent
29-33 ticks:	great
24-28 ticks:	good
less than 24 ticks:	keep practising. You'll get there!

Ten times table quiz

6 x 10 = ___ ☆	2 x 10 = ___ ☆	11 x 10 = ___ ☆
10 x 10 = ___ ☆	0 x 10 = ___ ☆	3 x 10 = ___ ☆
1 x 10 = ___ ☆	12 x 10 = ___ ☆	8 x 10 = ___ ☆
5 x 10 = ___ ☆	4 x 10 = ___ ☆	7 x 10 = ___ ☆
0 x 10 = ___ ☆	10 x 10 = ___ ☆	9 x 10 = ___ ☆
3 x 10 = ___ ☆	9 x 10 = ___ ☆	6 x 10 = ___ ☆
8 x 10 = ___ ☆	3 x 10 = ___ ☆	0 x 10 = ___ ☆
4 x 10 = ___ ☆	8 x 10 = ___ ☆	4 x 10 = ___ ☆
11 x 10 = ___ ☆	6 x 10 = ___ ☆	1 x 10 = ___ ☆
7 x 10 = ___ ☆	5 x 10 = ___ ☆	10 x 10 = ___ ☆
9 x 10 = ___ ☆	7 x 10 = ___ ☆	5 x 10 = ___ ☆
12 x 10 = ___ ☆	1 x 10 = ___ ☆	2 x 10 = ___ ☆
2 x 10 = ___ ☆	11 x 10 = ___ ☆	12 x 10 = ___ ☆

Total ticks ☆

Quiz comments

39 ticks:	congratulations! You're a whiz at this quiz!
34-38 ticks:	excellent
29-33 ticks:	great
24-28 ticks:	good
less than 24 ticks:	keep practising. You'll get there!

Eleven times table quiz

1 x 11 = ____ ☆	3 x 11 = ____ ☆	10 x 11 = ____ ☆
10 x 11 = ____ ☆	2 x 11 = ____ ☆	9 x 11 = ____ ☆
7 x 11 = ____ ☆	7 x 11 = ____ ☆	5 x 11 = ____ ☆
9 x 11 = ____ ☆	1 x 11 = ____ ☆	0 x 11 = ____ ☆
5 x 11 = ____ ☆	12 x 11 = ____ ☆	4 x 11 = ____ ☆
8 x 11 = ____ ☆	5 x 11 = ____ ☆	2 x 11 = ____ ☆
6 x 11 = ____ ☆	4 x 11 = ____ ☆	7 x 11 = ____ ☆
3 x 11 = ____ ☆	8 x 11 = ____ ☆	3 x 11 = ____ ☆
4 x 11 = ____ ☆	0 x 11 = ____ ☆	6 x 11 = ____ ☆
11 x 11 = ____ ☆	11 x 11 = ____ ☆	12 x 11 = ____ ☆
0 x 11 = ____ ☆	6 x 11 = ____ ☆	8 x 11 = ____ ☆
12 x 11 = ____ ☆	10 x 11 = ____ ☆	1 x 11 = ____ ☆
2 x 11 = ____ ☆	9 x 11 = ____ ☆	11 x 11 = ____ ☆

Total ticks ☆

Quiz comments

39 ticks:	congratulations! You're a whiz at this quiz!
34-38 ticks:	excellent
29-33 ticks:	great
24-28 ticks:	good
less than 24 ticks:	keep practising. You'll get there!

Twelve times table quiz

7 x 12 = ___ ☆		2 x 12 = ___ ☆		11 x 12 = ___ ☆
12 x 12 = ___ ☆		1 x 12 = ___ ☆		0 x 12 = ___ ☆
3 x 12 = ___ ☆		6 x 12 = ___ ☆		4 x 12 = ___ ☆
2 x 12 = ___ ☆		0 x 12 = ___ ☆		8 x 12 = ___ ☆
0 x 12 = ___ ☆		12 x 12 = ___ ☆		3 x 12 = ___ ☆
5 x 12 = ___ ☆		4 x 12 = ___ ☆		9 x 12 = ___ ☆
1 x 12 = ___ ☆		3 x 12 = ___ ☆		5 x 12 = ___ ☆
4 x 12 = ___ ☆		7 x 12 = ___ ☆		2 x 12 = ___ ☆
8 x 12 = ___ ☆		9 x 12 = ___ ☆		6 x 12 = ___ ☆
10 x 12 = ___ ☆		11 x 12 = ___ ☆		12 x 12 = ___ ☆
6 x 12 = ___ ☆		5 x 12 = ___ ☆		1 x 12 = ___ ☆
11 x 12 = ___ ☆		10 x 12 = ___ ☆		7 x 12 = ___ ☆
9 x 12 = ___ ☆		8 x 12 = ___ ☆		10 x 12 = ___ ☆

Total ticks ☆

Quiz comments

39 ticks:	congratulations! You're a whiz at this quiz!
34-38 ticks:	excellent
29-33 ticks:	great
24-28 ticks:	good
less than 24 ticks:	keep practising. You'll get there!

Super-duper square!

This super-duper square holds the answers to sums from the one times table through to the twelve times table. Wow!

For example, to discover the answer to 6 x 5, point to the six on the left side of the square and the 5 on the top of the square. Then draw your fingers in a straight line along the grid until they meet. Here you'll find your answer. That's right: 6 x 5 = 30
Now it's your turn!

x	0	1	2	3	4	5	6	7	8	9	10	11	12
0	0	0	0	0	0	0	0	0	0	0	0	0	0
1	0	1	2	3	4	5	6	7	8	9	10	11	12
2	0	2	4	6	8	10	12	14	16	18	20	22	24
3	0	3	6	9	12	15	18	21	24	27	30	33	36
4	0	4	8	12	16	20	24	28	32	36	40	44	48
5	0	5	10	15	20	25	30	35	40	45	50	55	60
6	0	6	12	18	24	30	36	42	48	54	60	66	72
7	0	7	14	21	28	35	42	49	56	63	70	77	84
8	0	8	16	24	32	40	48	56	64	72	80	88	96
9	0	9	18	27	36	45	54	63	72	81	90	99	108
10	0	10	20	30	40	50	60	70	80	90	100	110	120
11	0	11	22	33	44	55	66	77	88	99	110	121	132
12	0	12	24	36	48	60	72	84	96	108	120	132	144